ñF419748

I GOT MY MONEY IN MY PIGGY BANK

MONEY BOOK

Math Workbook for Kindergarten
Children's Money & Saving Reference

A PENNY
SAVED IS
A PENNY
EARNED.

TRACE
THE WORD

FRONT

BACK

TRACE THE WORDS BELOW.

penny penny

penny penny

NICKEL

FRONT

BACK

TRACE THE WORDS BELOW.

nickel nickel

nickel nickel

DIME

FRONT

BACK

TRACE THE WORDS BELOW.

dime dime

dime dime

FRONT

BACK

TRACE THE WORDS BELOW.

quarter quarter

quarter quarter

FRONT

BACK

TRACE THE WORDS BELOW.

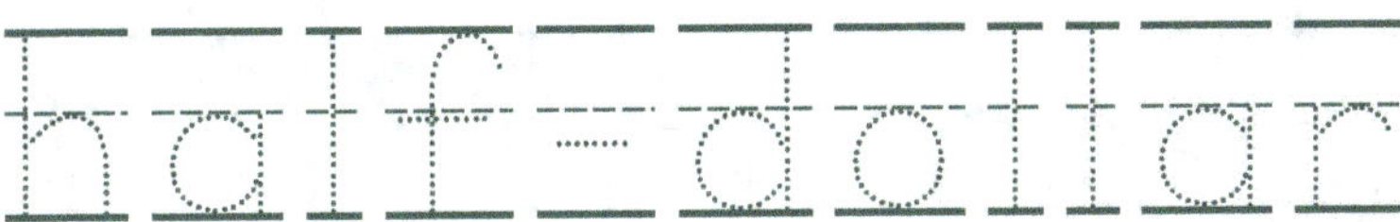

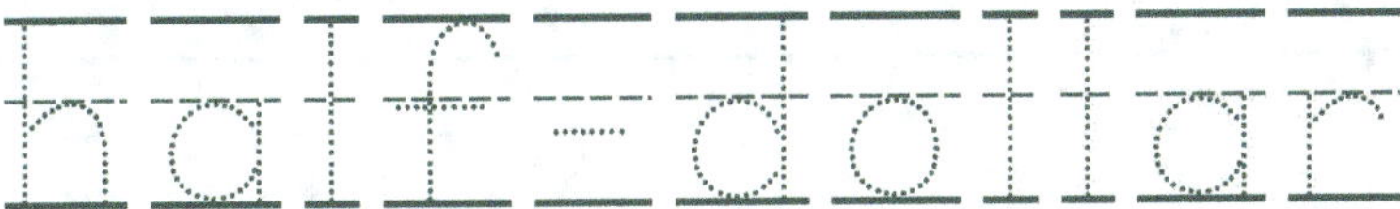

FRONT

BACK

TRACE THE WORDS BELOW.

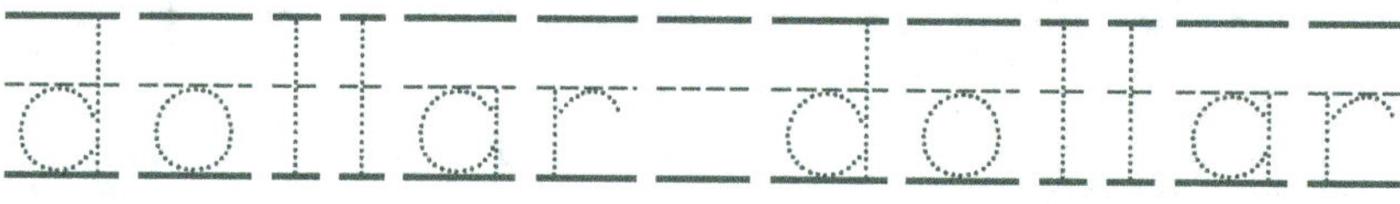

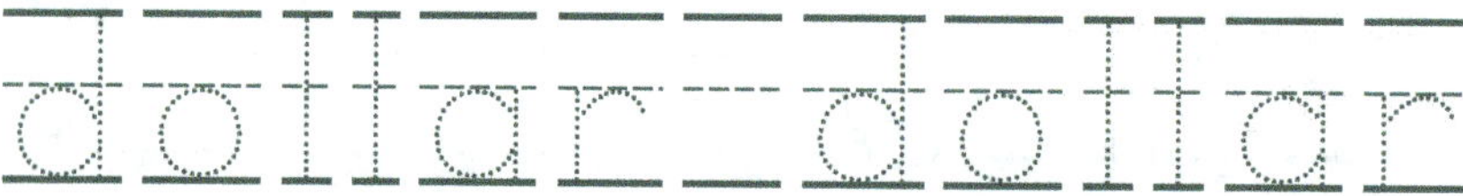

ODD ONE OUT

WHICH ONE IS DIFFERENT?
CIRCLE THE ODD ONE OUT

WHICH ONE IS DIFFERENT?
CIRCLE THE ODD ONE OUT

WHICH ONE IS DIFFERENT?
CIRCLE THE ODD ONE OUT

WHICH ONE IS DIFFERENT?
CIRCLE THE ODD ONE OUT

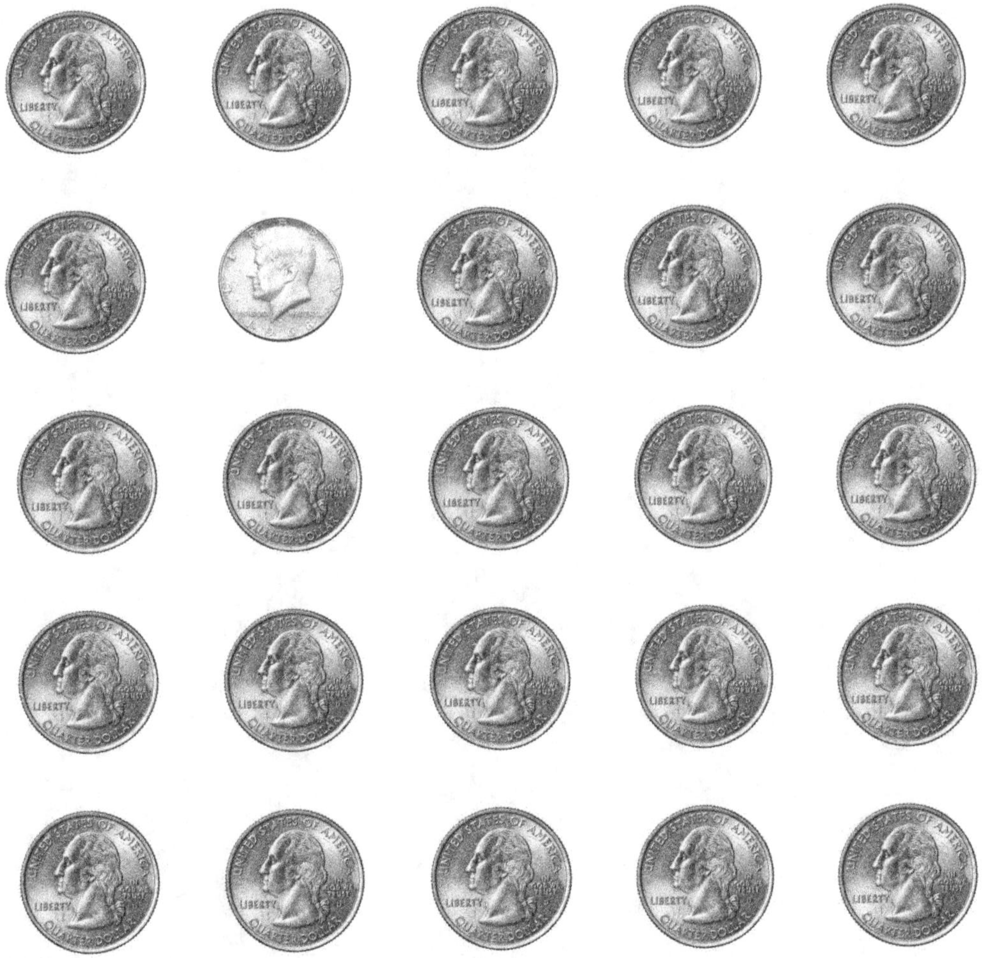

WHICH ONE IS DIFFERENT?
CIRCLE THE ODD ONE OUT

WHICH ONE IS DIFFERENT?
CIRCLE THE ODD ONE OUT

FIND THE MONEY

DRAW A CIRCLE AROUND ALL THE

1 CENT.

5 CENTS.

DRAW A CIRCLE AROUND ALL THE
10 CENTS.

DRAW A CIRCLE AROUND ALL THE
25 CENTS.

DRAW A CIRCLE AROUND ALL THE

50 CENTS.

DRAW A CIRCLE AROUND ALL THE
1 DOLLAR.

MONEY MATCHING

DRAW A LINE AND MATCH THE COIN WITH ITS VALUE.

25 ¢

10 ¢

1 ¢

DRAW A LINE AND MATCH THE COIN WITH ITS VALUE.

10 ¢

5 ¢

50 ¢

DRAW A LINE AND MATCH THE COIN WITH ITS VALUE.

50 ¢

$1

1 ¢

DRAW A LINE AND MATCH THE COIN WITH ITS VALUE.

5 ¢

$1

25 ¢

DRAW A LINE AND MATCH THE COIN WITH ITS VALUE.

1¢

10 ¢

50 ¢

DRAW A LINE FROM THE COIN IN THE LEFT COLUMN TO THE MATCHING COIN IN THE RIGHT COLUMN.

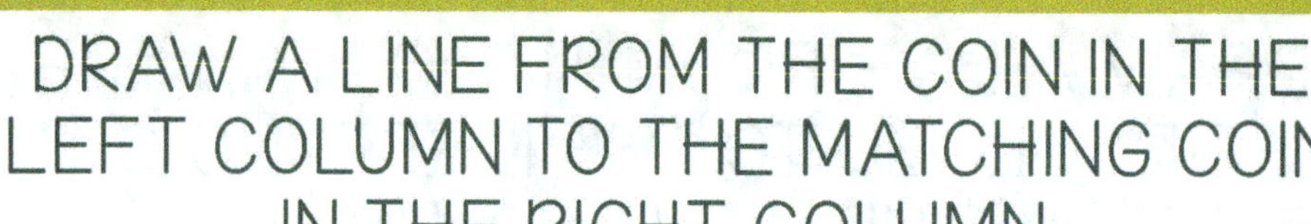

DRAW A LINE FROM THE COIN IN THE
LEFT COLUMN TO THE MATCHING COIN
IN THE RIGHT COLUMN.

DRAW A LINE FROM THE COIN IN THE LEFT COLUMN TO THE MATCHING COIN IN THE RIGHT COLUMN.

DRAW A LINE FROM THE COIN IN THE LEFT COLUMN TO THE MATCHING COIN IN THE RIGHT COLUMN.

DRAW A LINE FROM THE COIN IN THE LEFT COLUMN TO THE MATCHING COIN IN THE RIGHT COLUMN.

DRAW A LINE TO CONNECT EACH COIN ON THE LEFT TO ITS NAME ON THE RIGHT

penny

dollar

half-dollar

quarter

dime

penny

nickel

half-dollar

dime

DRAW A LINE TO CONNECT EACH COIN ON THE LEFT TO ITS NAME ON THE RIGHT

nickel

dollar

quarter

DRAW A LINE TO CONNECT EACH COIN ON THE LEFT TO ITS NAME ON THE RIGHT

dime

half-dollar

penny

DRAW A LINE TO MATCH THE PICTURE OF THE COINS TO THE CORRECT NAMES AND VALUES.

NAME	COIN	VALUE
quarter		1¢
dime		10¢
penny		25¢

NAME	COIN	VALUE
dollar		$1
nickel		50 ¢
half-dollar		5 ¢

DRAW A LINE TO MATCH
THE PICTURE OF THE COINS TO
THE CORRECT NAMES AND VALUES.

NAME	COIN	VALUE
nickel		10 ¢
half-dollar		5 ¢
dime		50 ¢

DRAW A LINE TO MATCH
THE PICTURE OF THE COINS TO
THE CORRECT NAMES AND VALUES.

NAME	COIN	VALUE
quarter		25 ¢
nickel		50 ¢
half-dollar		5 ¢

ANSWER KEYS

WHICH ONE IS DIFFERENT?
CIRCLE THE ODD ONE OUT

WHICH ONE IS DIFFERENT?
CIRCLE THE ODD ONE OUT

WHICH ONE IS DIFFERENT?
CIRCLE THE ODD ONE OUT

WHICH ONE IS DIFFERENT?
CIRCLE THE ODD ONE OUT

WHICH ONE IS DIFFERENT?
CIRCLE THE ODD ONE OUT

WHICH ONE IS DIFFERENT?
CIRCLE THE ODD ONE OUT

DRAW A CIRCLE AROUND ALL THE
1 CENT.

DRAW A CIRCLE AROUND ALL THE
5 CENTS.

DRAW A CIRCLE AROUND ALL THE
10 CENTS.

DRAW A CIRCLE AROUND ALL THE
25 CENTS.

DRAW A CIRCLE AROUND ALL THE
50 CENTS.

DRAW A CIRCLE AROUND ALL THE
1 DOLLAR.

DRAW A LINE AND MATCH THE COIN
WITH ITS VALUE.

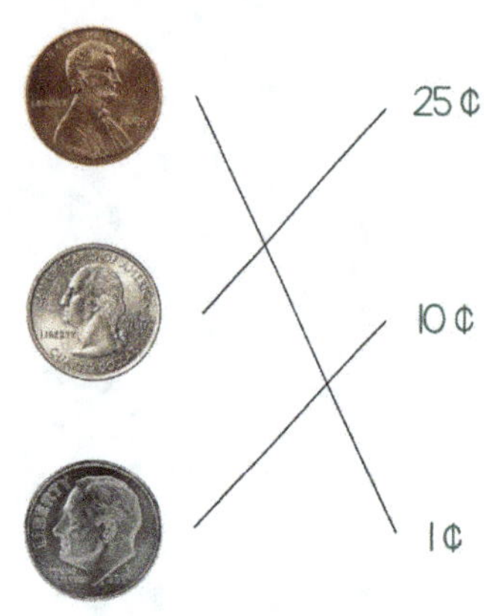

25 ¢

10 ¢

1 ¢

DRAW A LINE AND MATCH THE COIN
WITH ITS VALUE.

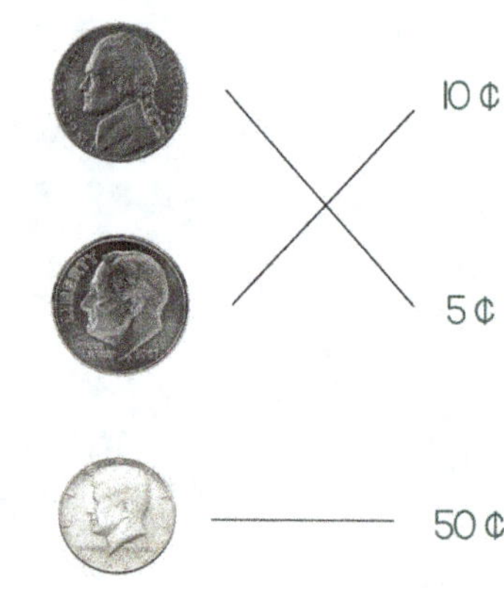

10 ¢

5 ¢

50 ¢

DRAW A LINE AND MATCH THE COIN
WITH ITS VALUE.

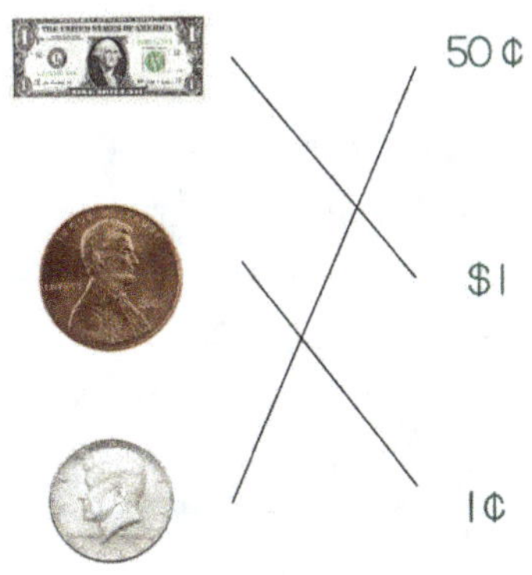

50 ¢

$1

1 ¢

DRAW A LINE AND MATCH THE COIN
WITH ITS VALUE.

5 ¢

$1

25 ¢

DRAW A LINE AND MATCH THE COIN WITH ITS VALUE.

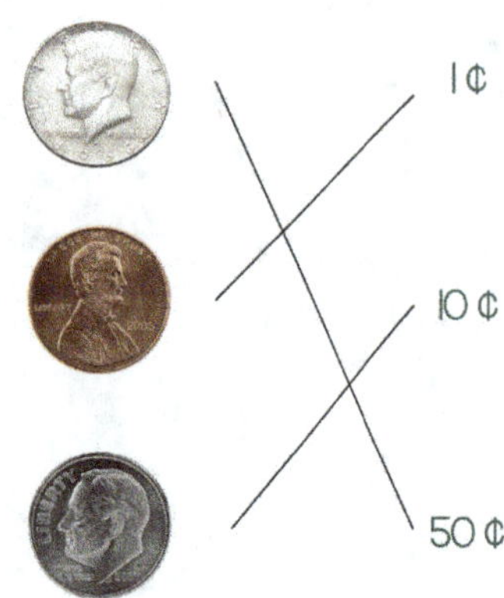

DRAW A LINE FROM THE COIN IN THE LEFT COLUMN TO THE MATCHING COIN IN THE RIGHT COLUMN.

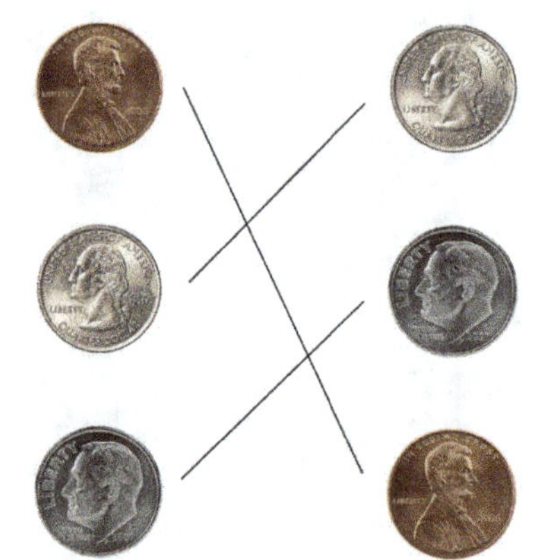

DRAW A LINE FROM THE COIN IN THE
LEFT COLUMN TO THE MATCHING COIN
IN THE RIGHT COLUMN.

DRAW A LINE FROM THE COIN IN THE
LEFT COLUMN TO THE MATCHING COIN
IN THE RIGHT COLUMN.

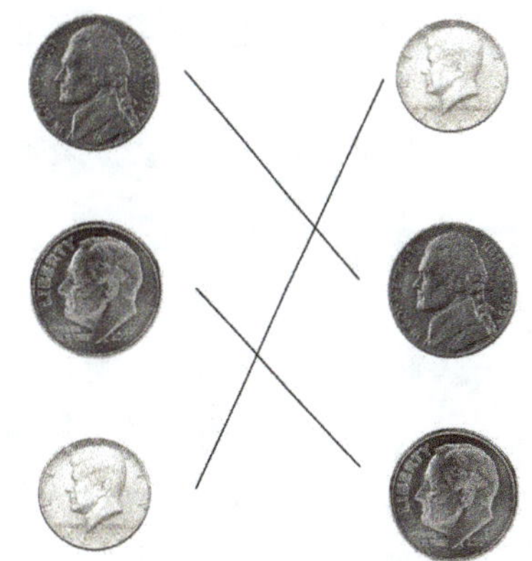

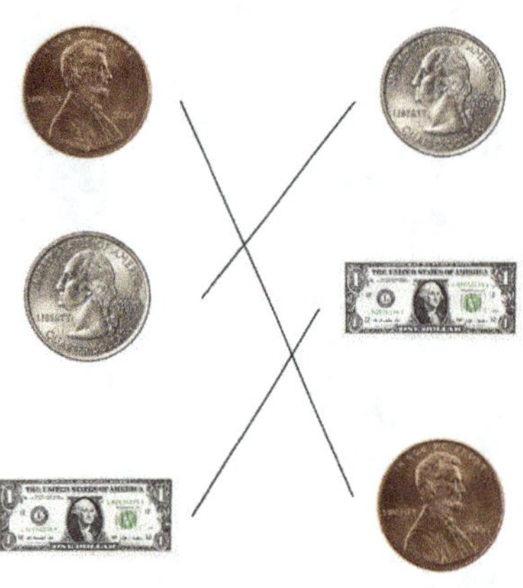

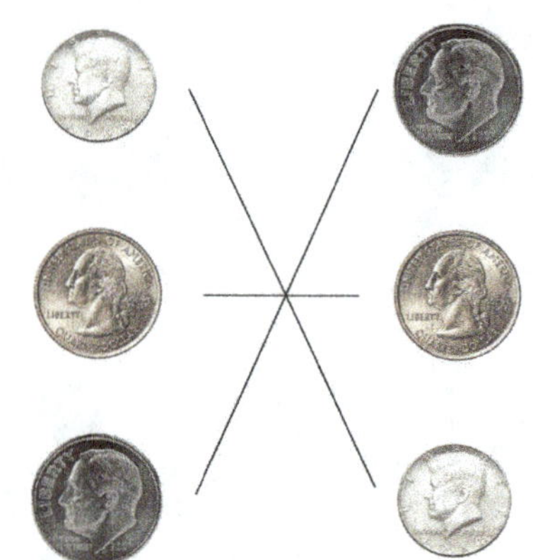

DRAW A LINE TO CONNECT EACH COIN ON THE LEFT TO ITS NAME ON THE RIGHT

penny

dollar

half-dollar

DRAW A LINE TO CONNECT EACH COIN ON THE LEFT TO ITS NAME ON THE RIGHT

quarter

dime

penny

DRAW A LINE TO CONNECT EACH COIN ON
THE LEFT TO ITS NAME ON THE RIGHT

nickel

half-dollar

dime

DRAW A LINE TO CONNECT EACH COIN ON
THE LEFT TO ITS NAME ON THE RIGHT

nickel

dollar

quarter

DRAW A LINE TO CONNECT EACH COIN ON
THE LEFT TO ITS NAME ON THE RIGHT

dime

half-dollar

penny

DRAW A LINE TO MATCH
THE PICTURE OF THE COINS TO
THE CORRECT NAMES AND VALUES.

NAME	COIN	VALUE
quarter		1¢
dime		10¢
penny		25¢

DRAW A LINE TO MATCH
THE PICTURE OF THE COINS TO
THE CORRECT NAMES AND VALUES.

NAME	COIN	VALUE

dollar  $1

nickel  50 ¢

half-dollar  5 ¢

DRAW A LINE TO MATCH
THE PICTURE OF THE COINS TO
THE CORRECT NAMES AND VALUES.

NAME	COIN	VALUE

nickel  10 ¢

half-dollar  5 ¢

dime 50 ¢

DRAW A LINE TO MATCH
THE PICTURE OF THE COINS TO
THE CORRECT NAMES AND VALUES.

NAME	COIN	VALUE
quarter		25 ¢
nickel		50 ¢
half-dollar		5 ¢

Visit
BABY PROFESSOR
EDUCATION KIDS
www.BabyProfessorBooks.com
to download Free Baby Professor eBooks
and view our catalog of new and exciting
Children's Books